SPORTS
HORSES

Stephanie Turnbull

A⁺

Smart Apple Media

Published by Smart Apple Media,
an imprint of Black Rabbit Books
P.O. Box 3263, Mankato, Minnesota, 56002
www.blackrabbitbooks.com

Designed by Hel James
Edited by Mary-Jane Wilkins

Cataloging-in-Publication Data is available from the Library of Congress

ISBN 978-1-62588-184-7

Photo acknowledgements
l = left, r = right; t = top, b = bottom
title page Perry Correll/Shutterstock.com; page 3 Alistair Scott/
Shutterstock; 4 Alexia Khruscheva/Shutterstock; 5 Anastasija Popova/
Shutterstock; 6 Ventura/ Shutterstock; 8-9 muzsy / Shutterstock.com;
11 olgaru79/Shutterstock.com; 12-13 pirita/Shutterstock; 14-15 Dennis
Donohue/Shutterstock; 16 Eduardo Rivero/Shutterstock.com;
17 EcoPrint/Shutterstock.com; 19 meirion matthias/Shutterstock.
com; 21 Christopher Meder/Shutterstock; 22 Anastasija Popova/
Shutterstock; 23 Kondrashov Mikhail Evgenevich
Cover scigelova/Shutterstock

Printed in China

DAD0055
032014
9 8 7 6 5 4 3 2 1

Contents

What are Sports Horses?

Sports horses can be any breed or size, as long as they are strong, healthy, and graceful.

Many sports horses are great jumpers. Some trek along tiring trails and others zigzag smoothly around obstacles.

They must be calm, brave, and easy to train—not shy or fiery-tempered!

Sports Gear

Sports horses wear a flat saddle. Extra straps called a breastplate keep the saddle from sliding around. Bandages or pads protect the horse's legs.

Riders wear a thick safety vest and a helmet.

Flat boots fit snugly into stirrups so that they don't slip.

Dressage

Dressage is a tricky competition that involves many careful, elegant moves. It's a bit like ballet for horses!

Horses may have to lift their legs up high…

Riders dress elegantly. Horses have neatly braided manes and polished hooves.

… or walk diagonally, or around in circles…

… and then trot on the spot or with their legs stretched.

Cross-country

In cross-country events, horses must jump over walls, fences, and ditches.

Horses must be fit and fast. Riders try to finish within a certain time, without falling, or missing jumps.

Show Jumping

Show jumping is fun to watch. Horses leap over colorful fences, trying not to knock down any poles.

Some fences are very wide.
Others have water under
them or are decorated
with flowers or fake bricks.

Horses do dressage,
cross-country and
show jumping in a
competition called
eventing.

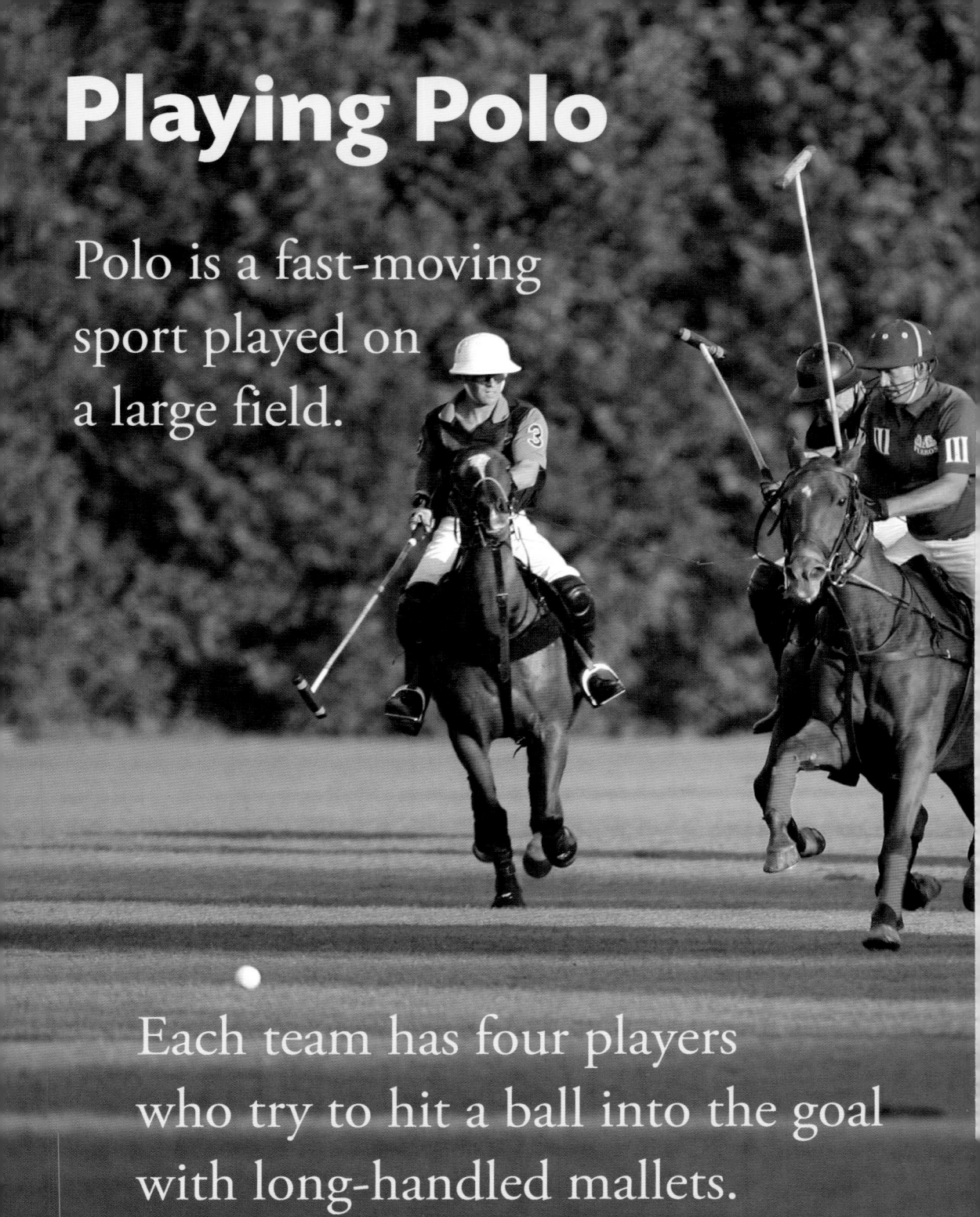

Playing Polo

Polo is a fast-moving sport played on a large field.

Each team has four players who try to hit a ball into the goal with long-handled mallets.

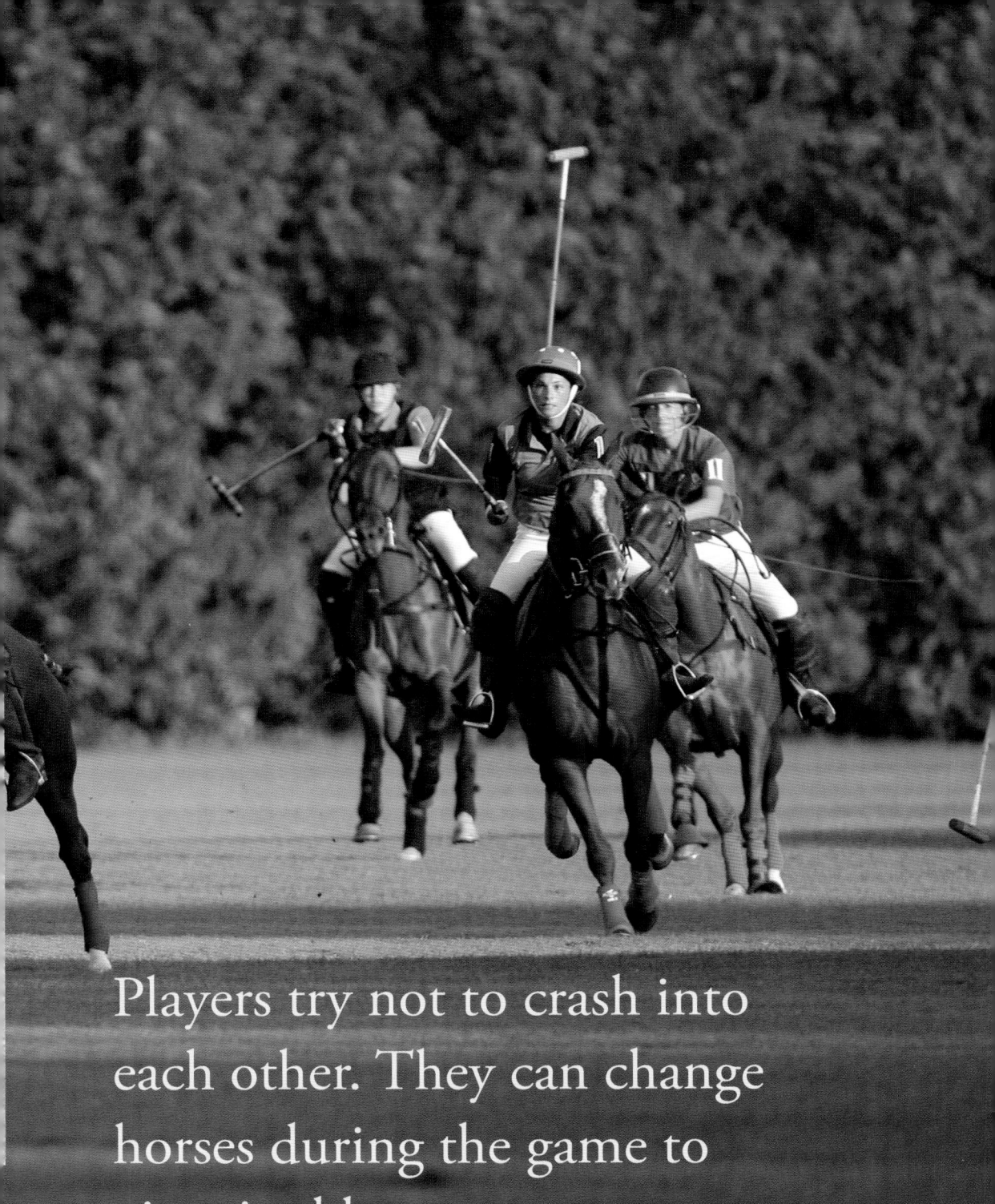

Players try not to crash into each other. They can change horses during the game to give tired horses a rest.

More Team Games

In horseball, riders throw a ball to each other and try to hurl it through a hoop.

The ball has handles to make it easy to catch—or grab from other players!

Polocrosse riders carry a net on a stick to catch and pass a rubber ball. They throw it between goal posts to score.

Carriage Driving

Some sports horses pull carriages around obstacle courses.

They sometimes work in teams of two or four horses.

A driver controls the horses. Helpers called grooms lean from side to side to keep the carriage upright.

The horses weave through cones and make tight turns around trees.

Muddy Marathons

Some strong horses take part in long-distance races.

Riders take a map and compass to find their way over hills, across streams, and through forests to the finish line.

Many long races have rest stops where vets check over the horses. Sometimes riders and horses camp out overnight.

Saddle Up!

Would you like to ride
horses in competitions?

Most riders begin by joining a riding club and take part in events called gymkhanas or O-Mok-See.

Training jumps have low poles that are gradually raised as horses learn to jump well.

Top sports horses and riders win lots of trophies, medals, and ribbons.

Useful Words

eventing A competition with three parts: dressage, cross-country, and show jumping. It often lasts three days.

gymkhana and **O-Mok-See** Fun races and games, usually for children and their ponies.

stirrups Loops hanging from a saddle where riders put their feet.

Index